Pray BEFORE READING

RYAN IVESDAL

CLAY BRIDGES
PRESS

Pray Before Reading
Copyright © 2024 by Ryan Ivesdal
Published by Clay Bridges Press in Houston, TX
www.ClayBridgesPress.com

Unless otherwise indicated, scripture quotations are taken from the (NASB) New American Standard Bible®, Copyright © 1960, 1971, 1977, 1995, 2020 by The Lockman Foundation. Used by permission. All rights reserved. www.lockman.org

Scripture quotations marked (ESV) are taken from the ESV® Bible (The Holy Bible, English Standard Version®), copyright © 2001 by Crossway, a publishing ministry of Good News Publishers. Used by permission. All rights reserved.

Scripture quotations marked (NIV) are taken from the Holy Bible, New International Version®, NIV®. Copyright ©1973, 1978, 1984, 2011 by Biblica, Inc.™ Used by permission of Zondervan. All rights reserved worldwide. www.zondervan.com The "NIV" and "New International Version" are trademarks registered in the United States Patent and Trademark Office by Biblica, Inc.™

Scripture quotations marked (NKJV) are taken from the New King James Version®. Copyright © 1982 by Thomas Nelson. Used by permission. All rights reserved.

ISBN: 978-1-68488-120-8 (Paperback)
ISBN: 978-1-68488-121-5 (Hardback)
eISBN: 978-1-68488-122-2 (eBook)

Special Sales: Most Clay Bridges titles are available in special quantity discounts. Custom imprinting or excerpting can also be done to fit special needs. Contact Clay Bridges at Info@ClayBridgesPress.com

Table of Contents

Introduction

The impetus for writing this book began when a friend asked me what the biblical number 666 meant. I took the question seriously because, for one, it's a biblical question, and anytime I'm dealing with the written Word of God, I want to be careful not to misrepresent God or His Word. I also understood that this question meant that my friend was genuinely interested in learning the truth. So, instead of answering off the top of my head, I decided to do in-depth research into the Book of Revelation and other parts of the Bible.

Fortunately, I had a fairly good understanding of the meaning and significance of the Scriptures surrounding 666, but even I was not prepared for the scope of what my research revealed. In *Pray Before Reading*, I will share what I learned about the importance of understanding the power of deception, explain how the Book of Revelation was written, decode some of its mysteries, and use this as a foundation for sharing the gospel.

Thank God for the Bible—this wonderful and amazing gift in which He reveals to us everything He wants us to know. It is my sincere hope that *Pray Before Reading* will glorify God. I am grateful to the person who asked this seemingly simple question. Otherwise, I might not have discovered another level of awe and wonder of the Lord God Almighty, Jesus Christ Himself.

Opening Prayer

Holy Father in Heaven,

Thank you for this opportunity to learn about You and to know You and Your plan for humanity. Bless the words written in this book and all who read it; may these words honor and glorify You. Use me today for Your purpose. Only one thing we ask, give us Your wisdom so that we may understand what we are about to study from Your word.

We know that when we ask for wisdom, You give freely because Your word tells us that *"if any of you lacks wisdom, let him ask of God, who gives to all generously and without reproach, and it will be given to him"* (James 1:5).

Jesus, in Matthew 7:7–11, You said:

> *Ask, and it will be given to you; seek, and you will find; knock, and it will be opened to you. For everyone who asks receives, and the one who seeks finds, and to the one who knocks it will be opened. Or what person is there among you who, when his*

son asks for a loaf of bread, will give him a stone? Or if he asks for a fish, he will not give him a snake, will he? So if you, despite being evil, know how to give good gifts to your children, how much more will your Father who is in heaven give good things to those who ask Him!

Thank You, Father, for giving us this blessing. We ask for wisdom and understanding and the humility to accept what You reveal to us through Your word. In the name above all names, the King of kings and Lord of lords, Jesus Christ. May Your kingdom come and Your will be done on earth as it is in Heaven.

Amen.

The Truth about Deception

Before we explore how the Book of Revelation was written and decode some of its mysteries, we need to fully comprehend the concept of deception and the spirit behind it. The most important thing to comprehend, the most important word to understand in all of this, is *deception*. Deception is Satan's most deadly weapon; it is the greatest death trap Satan has, and he is very good at using it. Satan is the great deceiver:

> *So the great dragon was cast out, that serpent of old, called the Devil and Satan, who deceives the whole world; he was cast to the earth, and his angels were cast out with him.*
>
> —Revelation 12:9 NKJV

He will do anything in his power to deceive people. Anything! The Bible reveals that Satan gives power to certain people to perform great signs and wonders. He has the power to deceive the entire world except for born-again believers. Everyone. This is nothing new; he has been deceiving people ever since the garden in Eden when he deceived Eve:

> And the LORD God said to the woman, "What is this you have done?" The woman said, "The serpent deceived me, and I ate."
> —Genesis 3:13 NKJV

Throughout history, he has used signs and wonders to deceive people. Both the Old Testament and the New Testament record how relentless Satan is at deceiving people, even the apostles. Perhaps the most well-known example of an apostle being deceived is found in Mathew16:23:

> But He [Jesus] turned and said to Peter, "Get behind Me, Satan! You are a stumbling block to Me; for you are not setting your mind on God's purposes, but men's."

Peter shows us what can happen if we let Satan sway us from following Jesus's teaching closely. This applies to anyone who gets in the way of the work of God, like evangelizing. For example, let's say you mailed a letter to someone, trying to reach them for Christ, trying to evangelize them, but their spouse, not wanting confrontation or fearing an argument or conflict, snatches it out of the mailbox before the person gets a chance to see it. In this case, the spouse is standing in the way or being a stumbling block to God's work. They think they are doing the right thing by not allowing the person to read the letter or even know about it, but actually, what they have done is selfish. They are saving themselves from an uncomfortable situation by choosing peace over salvation. In effect, they are choosing comfort over Christ, which is why Jesus gave this stern warning:

> *Do not think that I came to bring peace on the earth; I did not come to bring peace, but a sword. For I came to* turn a man against his father, and a daughter against her mother, and a daughter-in-law against her mother-in-law; *and* a person's enemies will be the members of his household. *The one who loves father or mother more than Me is not worthy of Me; and the one who loves son or daughter more than Me is not worthy of Me. And the one who does not take his cross and follow after Me is not worthy of Me. The one who has found his life will lose it, and the one who has lost his life on My account will find it.*
>
> —Matthew 10:34–39

In similar fashion, deception plays a key role in trying to hamper the spread of the gospel in the parable of the sower explained in Matthew 13 Verses 19 and 22:

> *When anyone hears the word of the kingdom and does not understand it, the evil one comes and snatches away what has been sown in his heart. This is the one sown with seed beside the road. . . . And the one sown with seed among the thorns, this is the one who hears the word, and the anxiety of the world and the deceitfulness of wealth choke the word, and it becomes unfruitful.*

Likewise, Satan tried to deceive two of the disciples to get them to call down fire from Heaven to kill people.

> *And when His disciples James and John saw this, they said, "Lord, do You want us to command fire to come down from heaven and consume them, just as Elijah did?" But He turned and rebuked them, and said, "You do not know what manner of spirit you are of. For the Son of Man did not come to destroy men's lives but to save them." And they went to another village.*
>
> —Luke 9:54–56 NKJV

When we discuss the book of Revelation later, we will meet a man who has the power to call down fire from Heaven, and he does it for all the world to see. However, do not be fooled by signs. As we noted above, Satan has been given the power to perform signs and wonders.

Yes, God did use fire in the Old Testament as a sign. First Kings 18:20–40 records the story of the time that Elijah challenged 450 prophets of Baal to see if their so-called god was real. He mocked them when their fake god didn't show up. Elijah's God did show up—in a flame of fire and burned up the offering.

The point of this is to say that it's not about the sign; it is about what it is being used for. Satan always uses signs and miracles to deceive people, or as in the case of Roman Catholicism, to keep people in their deep state of deception. A dear friend who is a staunch Roman Catholic approached me recently excited to tell me that not long ago, someone they knew took communion bread from the tabernacle in a Roman Catholic church to have it tested, and they discovered that it contained human DNA, like that of the human heart. Wow! Satan is very, very powerful. How do we know this is not a sign from God to somehow prove Himself or to legitimize Roman Catholic practices? The answer is found in the Book of Matthew:

Then some of the scribes and Pharisees answered, saying, "Teacher, we want to see a sign from You." But He answered and said to them, "An evil and adulterous generation seeks after a sign, and no sign will be given to it except the sign of the prophet Jonah."
—Matthew 12:38–39 NKJV

Satan is so powerful that even Michael the archangel did not dare to rebuke him but said to him, *"The Lord rebuke you"* (Jude 1:9)! That's just one example of the great lengths to which Satan will go to deceive people and keep them in his trap. His deceptions are very dangerous.

When the disciples asked Jesus to tell them when the end of the age would come and what would be the sign of His coming, His response was direct and specific:

Now as He sat on the Mount of Olives, the disciples came to Him privately, saying, "Tell us, when will these things be? And what will be the sign of Your coming, and of the end of the age?" And Jesus answered and said to them: "Take heed that no one deceives you. For many will come in My name, saying, 'I am the Christ,' and will deceive many."
—Matthew 24:3–5 NKJV

Notice that Jesus didn't say to store up food and ammo. He didn't say prepare to bug out somewhere. He said, *"Take heed that no one deceives you."* He knew how things would be in our time. He knew that reality and truth would become increasingly subjective. Why is it so important to understand and recognize deception? Because those who are deceived don't know they are being deceived. That's the essence of deception. They need someone to tell them, but most Christians are not willing to stand firm against the deceptive traps people are caught in and tell them the truth. That's why Satan loves deception so much and why he loves weak Christians.

The Basics of Biblical Prophecy

Understanding Prophetic Writing

The events of the end-times or the Tribulation culminate in the Great Tribulation, during which the full force of God's wrath and righteous judgment against sinful man will be poured out on the entire world. The Tribulation will be the last seven years of human history. To provide some context for the chapters that follow, this section outlines the most significant events of this period.

Many prophetic events take place to kick off the Great Tribulation, and these events happen in rapid succession. First, a great war breaks out in heaven between Michael the archangel and Satan (Revelation 12:7–9). Satan is cast down to earth like lightning (Luke 10:18), and a war breaks out on earth (Ezekiel 38). The rapture of believers takes place, but no one knows the day or hour (Matthew 24:36–51) when that will happen.

Then, the Antichrist, who is the one-world government ruler, is revealed (Revelation 6:2). He brings peace and makes a seven-year covenant with the Jewish nation, after which the Jews begin building a temple in Jerusalem (Daniel 9:27). Three and a half years into the Tribulation, the temple opens for operation. But the Antichrist breaks his promise of peace with the Jews, kicks them out of the temple, and sets himself up in the temple to be worshiped as if he is God (Matthew 24:15).

He gets a severe head wound, and the entire world thinks he has died (Revelation 13:3). This gives rise to the one-world religious leader who has all the power and authority of the first ruler, the Antichrist (Revelation 13:12), bringing a false peace and unity to the entire world (1 Thessalonians 5:3). The one-world religious leader becomes the head not only of religion but of all the world's political systems; he creates a one-world currency that is linked to the mark of 666 that everyone is required to have on their bodies. The mark will be the only way they can buy and sell, and it will be an expression of honor to the "dead" first leader because the mark represents him (Revelation 13:16–18). He has satanic supernatural power and supposedly raises the one-world government ruler from the dead (Revelation 13:13–14). This deception fools the entire world into thinking that the government leader has been brought back to life, and they will worship him as a god (Revelation 13:14–15). The "resurrected" government leader and the nations that fully support him reject the one-world religious leader, strip him of his power, and kill him and his followers (Revelation 17:16–17).

By this time, two-thirds of the world's population will have died (Zechariah 13:8), and extreme climate change will have caused devastating effects on all plants, animals, and humans on a global scale (Ezekiel 5:12). Earthquakes (Revelation 16:18), volcanic eruptions (Revelation 8:8) that block out the sun (Ezekiel 32:7–8 and Revelation 8:12), tsunamis (Revelation 8:13), hailstorms (Revelation 16:21), wildfires, death, and disease cause plagues of every kind imaginable (Revelation 16), turning the planet into an uninhabitable cesspool of suffering, filth, and death.

It is at this point that Jesus returns; otherwise, all life would be lost (Matthew 24:22).

Seeing the World from the Supernatural Perspective

The Book of Revelation is a supernatural book both in its authorship and in its content. This New Testament book gives the reader a sneak peek into the supernatural realm. The Bible—specifically the book of Revelation—is the only divinely written book that reveals, at least in part, the amazing and limitless reality of another dimension or what the Bible calls "the heavens."

The Bible teaches that there are two realms. First, there is our current reality—the natural, physical world, which is bound by natural laws of time and physics. The second realm is the greater reality—the supernatural, spiritual dimension, which is not bound by the laws of the physical world. In this realm, everything is revealed as it is in the spirit, which produces a greater, truer reality, not confined by time, or gravity, or physical laws; this realm is governed directly by God.

The spiritual realm can be a difficult concept for humans to comprehend because we are constrained to think in terms of the environment in which we live. We may never fully understand the spiritual realm as long as we exist in our natural bodies. Even after this life is over and we, who are being saved, enter this spiritual realm, also called the heavens, we will spend eternity discovering the vastness of the limitless imagination of God.

In addition to John, who wrote the book of Revelation, other New Testament writers give us tidbits of information about this alternate reality, but it's very limited. Luke records the stoning of Stephen, who was the first New Testament martyr. As he is dying, Stephen tells us what he sees just before he enters Heaven. As he's being stoned for preaching in the name of Jesus Christ, he gives us a glimpse into Heaven:

> Now when they heard this, they were infuriated, and they began gnashing their teeth at him. But he, being full of the Holy Spirit, looked intently into heaven and saw the glory of God, and Jesus standing at the right hand of God; and he said, "Behold, I see the heavens opened and the Son of Man standing at the right hand of God."
>
> —Acts 7:54–56

These verses do not give us a way of understanding the spiritual realm, but they do give us a vivid eyewitness account of Jesus being where He said He would be. Of course, the religious leaders absolutely hated hearing this because they hated Jesus and could not even conceive of Him being at the right hand of God. That's because they were not of God but of Satan; they were deceived. You may see this kind of hostility from some who hear the Word of God; if the Word infuriates them, you know they are not of God but of Satan.

The Bible includes the Apostle Paul's testimony about the heavens or what he calls Paradise. He, like Stephen, was stoned for preaching in the name of Jesus Christ. During his first missionary journey, Paul was stoned by his opponents in Lystra, and because they thought he had died, they dragged his "dead" body outside the city wall so it would not contaminate the city according to Jewish law (Acts 14:19–28). Of course, Paul recovered and continued to preach the gospel among the Gentiles.

> *But Jews came from Antioch and Iconium, and having won over the crowds, they stoned Paul and dragged him out of the city, thinking that he was dead. But while the disciples stood around him, he got up and entered the city. The next day he left with Barnabas for Derbe.*
> —Acts 14:19–20 NASB2020

Later, in his ministry, the Apostle Paul describes his incredible heavenly experience, which he mentions briefly:

> *I know a man in Christ, who fourteen years ago—whether in the body I do not know, or out of the body I do not know, God knows—such a man was caught up to the third heaven. And I know how such a man—whether in the body or apart from the body I do not know, God knows—was caught up into Paradise and heard inexpressible words, which a man is not permitted to speak. On behalf of such a man, I will boast, but on my own behalf, I will not boast, except regarding my weaknesses. For if I do wish to boast, I*

*will not be foolish, for I will be speaking the truth; but
I refrain from this, so that no one will credit me with
more than he sees in me or hears from me.*
—2 Corinthians 12:2–6 NASB2020

Here, Paul is talking about himself. Not wanting in any way to
boast or give any hint of being proud, he speaks of himself in the
third person. This is unlike any of the false claims we hear today
from people who say they have been to Heaven and come back to
tell about the experience. Everyone who makes this false claim of
dying and going to Heaven or hell and back is doing it for money
or to gain popularity. The source of these stories is nothing more
than a good imagination, a demon encounter, or both. Satan is
simply feeding them misinformation. How can we be sure about
this? Because we have the words of Scripture to confirm the truth:

*Just as people are destined to die once, and after that
to face judgment, so Christ was sacrificed once to take
away the sins of many; and he will appear a second
time, not to bear sin, but to bring salvation to those
who are waiting for him.*
—Hebrews 9:27–28 NIV

This is why it is so important to understand that Paul did not
die from the stoning but was raptured, which means to be caught
up. Otherwise, there would be a contradiction in Scripture, and
Scripture never contradicts itself. Paul was the one who was
caught up in Acts 14:19, as he described later in 2 Corinthians
12:3–4. The Greek word used for "caught up" is "harpazo"; its
equivalent translation is the word *raptured*. Paul was raptured

into Paradise and saw and heard things too inexpressible for words. When Paul came back from being raptured, he couldn't express what he heard because, first of all, it wasn't given to him to interpret; that's the most important reason. Second, he had other things going on in his life that didn't allow him time to sit and ponder what he had just experienced. He was literally running for his life much of the time.

From Stephen's account, we get confirmation that Jesus is at the right hand of God; from Paul's account, we get, "I can't tell you" what I saw. As limited as their accounts are, they are significant in letting us know what we will see when we die. Jesus will be there, and the environment will be mind-blowing. How mind-blowing? Well, just stay tuned; that's where the book of Revelation comes in.

In the book of Revelation, John puts into words for us what Paul could not. Why was John able to put his vision into words and write it down, but Paul couldn't? First, by the time John received *"the revelation of Jesus Christ,"* he was no longer busy with his duty of fulfilling "The Great Commission" or other things that could distract him from what God wanted to reveal to him. He was very old; all the other disciples had been put to death at this point, and he was the last remaining disciple. His time of evangelizing and spreading the good news everywhere is basically over. He was exiled to *"the island called Patmos because of the word of God and the testimony of Jesus"* (Revelation 1:9). So, he was in the perfect position to be used by God. God could take him away in the Spirit, and no one would even notice, and that's exactly what happened to John. John was raptured away in the Spirit, just like Paul was.

After this, I looked, and there before me was a door standing open in heaven. And the voice I had first heard speaking to me like a trumpet said, "Come up here, and I will show you what must take place after this." At once, I was in the Spirit, and there before me was a throne in heaven with someone sitting on it.

—Revelation 4:1–2 NIV

Second, and most importantly, strictly speaking, John is not the author of the book of Revelation; these are not John's words. John is writing what Jesus is telling him to write. The book of Revelation is being dictated by Jesus through His angel to John (Revelation 1:19).

The Revelation of Jesus Christ, which God gave Him to show to His bond-servants, the things which must soon take place; and He sent and communicated it by His angel to His bond-servant John, who testified to the word of God and to the testimony of Jesus Christ, everything that he saw.

—Revelation 1:1–2

So, we don't need to worry about anything being lost in translation, or misinterpretation, or human exaggeration. Nothing is left to John's imagination to try to work out. Thankfully, the text is given to him to write, and even in some cases, he's told what not to write. The book of Revelation is not written in a dramatic way just to give it some flare and make it captivating or mysterious. It is an eyewitness account.

The book of Revelation is prophetic. The layout of the book follows the principles of biblical prophecy, which comes in three parts. Thus, the content is written with a focus on what was (past), what is (present), and what is to come (future). Here's just one example:

> *The beast that you saw was, and is not, and is about to come up out of the abyss and go to destruction. And those who live on the earth, whose names have not been written in the book of life from the foundation of the world, will wonder when they see the beast, that he was, and is not, and will come.*
>
> —Revelation 17:8

There, we have an example of past (*"the beast that you saw"*), present (*"and is not"*), and future (*"is about to come"*).

Four Interpretive Approaches to Revelation

Bible scholars have identified four main ways to approach interpreting the book of Revelation:

- **Preterist.** Those who hold this view believe that prophecies are metaphors, pictures, types, and symbols pointing to something but not necessarily literal events.
- **Historicist.** Historicists believe that prophecies are fulfilled as a pattern throughout history. They believe that some prophecies were fulfilled as a part of past history, some are being fulfilled today, and some are yet to be fulfilled.
- **Idealist.** Idealists believe that all prophecy has already been fulfilled, and they believe that biblical events support this claim.

- **Futurist**. Futurists believe that some prophecies may have happened, but they believe that most prophecies are yet to be fulfilled.

I will not go into detail about these views here but suffice it to say that none of these views completely contradicts the others; neither does one approach cancel out the others. The book of Revelation proves all of them to be correct to some degree. I don't subscribe exclusively to one of these views because they all have some truth in them, but no view provides a complete explanation for prophecy. For instance, the historicist view recognizes a pattern of prophetic events but overlooks the fact that some prophecies happen repeatedly, and this view does not account for the fact that prophecies can also be metaphors, types, and pictures pointing to something greater than themselves. Yes, prophecies can be metaphors, pictures, and types pointing to something, but they are also literal events that take place. Yes, prophecies have been fulfilled throughout history as literal events, and many prophecies were fulfilled in the past, but not all prophecies have taken place yet. Many more prophecies are yet to be fulfilled.

Revelation is written like one of those movies that starts in the present, then goes into the future, then back to the past, then back to the present. The book of Revelation flows back and forth through time seamlessly and simultaneously, which is where a lot of people can get lost and confused. Revelation gives us a hint of what it's like not being constricted and conformed by time. The supernatural realm is outside of time.

Unlocking Some of Revelation's Mysteries

Using an Analogy

Understanding the book of Revelation can be challenging because it deals almost exclusively with the supernatural realm, which is outside of time. An analogy might help. Let's assume that you're watching a movie at an Imax theater. You know, the ones where the movie screen is like a big dome; it's over your head, in front of you, and down both sides. Imagine you're lying on the floor looking up, and on the giant screen is not a movie but the entire history of all creation being played out. And it's displayed so that if you look to your left, you see history past; if you look straight ahead, you see history present; if you look to your right, you see history future—all playing simultaneously.

All you have to do is look in different directions, and you can see all of history—all creation, seamlessly. And if you look straight ahead, you can see with your peripheral vision, all of it at the same time, seamlessly and simultaneously. Imagine seeing all of history like that and trying to describe it. Now imagine seeing all of history like that from the spiritual perspective but seeing everything in greater reality than it exists in the physical world and then trying to describe the experience. Now you know why Paul had no words, and you can see the challenge that John faced as he tried to record what he was seeing from a spiritual perspective. This would literally be mind-blowing, and only by the power of God could it be put into words for John to write down. This is how John, being in the Spirit, could see, hear, and observe past, present, and future events taking place right in front of him simultaneously.

Think of the experience like viewing a movie. With a movie, you can fast-forward to the end, rewind to the beginning, skip to the middle, or anywhere in between. What makes it possible for us to do that? Because the movie has already been created and is done. Production is over, and the finished product is available. While production is underway, you can't fast-forward to see the end because it hasn't happened yet. Or maybe the producer had a brilliant ending and hasn't written the beginning or the middle yet, so we wouldn't be able to see those parts because they haven't been created yet. God's "movie" of creation from beginning to end is complete. So, in the book of Revelation, human history is revealed to John in its entirety, and the producer, God, can fast-forward, rewind, or play the past, present, or future because human history has all already been completed—at least, in the spiritual realm.

How do we know this is true? There are a few clues in the Bible. For example, Isaiah 46:9–10 says:

Remember the former things of old, for I am God, and there is no other; I am God, and there is none like Me, declaring the end from the beginning, and from ancient times things that are not yet done, saying, "My counsel shall stand, and I will do all My pleasure."

And John sees and reports several dispensations of time in an instant. He sees and reports:

- The fall of Satan (he was cast down to earth and his angels with him)
- The birth of Christ (the woman clothed in the sun)
- The church period (first three chapters)
- The rapture, tribulation, return of Christ, and thousand-year reign of Christ and beyond

This all happens without any passage of time. It was all playing out before John in just the "time" it took him to write it all out, but he was observing all these events instantaneously, simultaneously, and seamlessly.

Another reason we know that these things have already happened, at least in the spiritual world, is that throughout the Bible, you will notice that past tense is used where we would usually expect present tense to be used. That is, future events are spoken about in the present tense as if they have already happened in the past. This is especially prevalent in prophetic books such as Revelation.

Third, as we read earlier in Revelation 17:8, the Bible says that names were written in the Lamb's Book of Life before the foundation of the earth or from the creation of the world.

> *All inhabitants of the earth will worship the beast—*
> *all whose names have not been written in the Lamb's*
> *book of life, the Lamb who was slain from the creation*
> *of the world.*
> —Revelation 13:8 NIV

That simple statement is another example of what we are talking about. It has the past, the present, and the future—all in one short verse. The *"inhabitants of the earth"* (present), *"worship the beast"* (future), "names written" (past), "the crucifixion" (middle history), and *"slain before creation of the world"* (back to the past).

The names written in the Lamb's Book of Life are the redeemed, the saved, the born again, and the overcomers; their names were written in the book before time began. Thinking back to the movie analogy, we can say that the casting call is already done. You can't walk up to the set midway through production and ask to be added in. The producer, God, already called and elected who is in and who is out.

> *For those whom He foreknew, He also predestined to*
> *become conformed to the image of His Son, so that*
> *He would be the firstborn among many brothers and*
> *sisters; and these whom He predestined, He also called;*
> *and these whom He called, He also justified; and these*
> *whom He justified, He also glorified.*
> —Romans 8:29–30

In the Gospels of John and Matthew, Jesus says:

- *"You did not choose Me, but I chose you and appointed you that you should go and bear fruit, and that your fruit should remain, that whatever you ask the Father in My name He may give you"* (John 15:16 NKJV).
- *"For many are called, but few are chosen"* (Matthew 22:14 NKJV).

In the book of Acts, we get this good news for Gentile believers: Notice the use of the past perfect tense verb "had been." This indicates an action or event that was completed in the past before another action or event in the present. In this instance, the past perfect tense indicates that certain people were already appointed to eternal life before this event happened. But now, because of this event (i.e., the Gentiles hearing the gospel), their salvation may be made complete because they heard and believed—bringing God's perfect plan of redemption, which started before the foundation of the earth, to fruition. This is why the work of evangelism or proclaiming the good news is so vitally important.

> *When the Gentiles heard this, they began rejoicing and glorifying the word of the Lord; and all who had been appointed to eternal life believed.*
> —Acts 13:48

Why does it say in this verse, "they began rejoicing"? Because they "heard, the word of the Lord". They needed to hear in order to believe.

For "everyone who calls on the name of the Lord will be saved." How then will they call on him in whom they have not believed? And how are they to believe in him of whom they have never heard? And how are they to hear without someone preaching? And how are they to preach unless they are sent? As it is written, "How beautiful are the feet of those who preach the good news!" But they have not all obeyed the gospel. For Isaiah says, "Lord, who has believed what he has heard from us?" So faith comes from hearing, and hearing through the word of Christ.

—Romans 10:13-17 ESV

The Gentiles in Acts 13:48, were "predestined" by God, as is says in Romans 8:30, "to eternal life" and "called". What does "called" mean? That is the work of the "preacher" or evangelist whom God uses to proclaim "the good news" concerning Christ, that's the calling. Man's will in God's great plan of redemption is the willingness of the born again believer to go forth and preach the gospel to all. This is The Great Commission. Not all believers are willing to do this; however, it is up to us the true believers to be willing to do the work we are commanded to do. Those who hear and believe have been called by God through His workers, the ones who proclaim the gospel, in order that they may be saved in the perfect timing of Gods plan of redemption, which He designed before time began. By this process God is able to work out the rest of the verse in Romans 8:30. Once they have heard and believe, they are instantly "justified" by the atoning sacrifice of Jesus Christ, and then in heaven they are "glorified" for eternity. This is the reconciliation of Gods plan of redemption, predestination, and mans will.

However, there are those whose name will be blotted out of the book. These are the stand-ins, the extras, the ones who want to be a part of the production but are not fully committed. They are the ones who are only there for the benefits but not for the commitment.

> *I testify to everyone who hears the words of the prophecy of this book: if anyone adds to them, God will add to him the plagues that are written in this book, and if anyone takes away from the words of the book of this prophecy, God will take away his part from the tree of life and from the holy city, which are written in this book.*
>
> —Revelation 22:18–19

In the NASB version of Revelation 22:18–19 shown above, the "Book of Life" is called the "Tree of Life." Other translations of this text say the "Book of Life" instead of the "Tree of Life." It seems as though these terms can be used interchangeably.

> *For I testify to everyone who hears the words of the prophecy of this book: If anyone adds to these things, God will add to him the plagues that are written in this book; and if anyone takes away from the words of the book of this prophecy, God shall take away his part from the Book of Life, from the holy city, and from the things which are written in this book.*
>
> —Revelation 22:18–19 NKJV

These are the false Christians. The religious. The cults. The ones who claim the name of Christ to be their own but are not "born again." Only false believers would dare tamper with the Word of God to make it fit into their lifestyles and belief systems despite the warning here in Chapter 22. Such people may have false confidence about their salvation; they may think they are in because they say they believe even though their belief is not based on true knowledge. These are false Christians—the ones who claim the name of Christ as their own but are not "born again."

> *Brothers and sisters, my heart's desire and my prayer to God for them is for their salvation. For I testify about them that they have a zeal for God, but not in accordance with knowledge. For not knowing about God's righteousness and seeking to establish their own, they did not subject themselves to the righteousness of God. For Christ is the end of the Law for righteousness to everyone who believes.*
>
> —Romans 10:1–4

Why does this passage say they have a zeal for God but not according to knowledge? Because remember, these are the ones who tamper with the Word of God. These are the religions, denominations, or churches that take away and add to God's Word to make it fit their agenda or belief system. For example, Roman Catholicism elevates its traditions over the Bible. Can you think of someone who has a zeal for God—someone who appears to be super religious and devoted to a system or church attendance but doesn't understand the Bible? Or you may know someone who has been through a rite of passage such as confirmation or infant baptism, which gives them a sense of completion, so they only show up at church on Christmas and Easter. When churches elevate traditions or anything above or equal to the Bible, they are no longer teaching the true and full Word of God; they are teaching their own interpretation of the Bible mixed with man-made traditions. This results in false knowledge about God and a misunderstanding of the righteousness of God because they manipulated the Word of God. This results in them seeking their own righteousness instead of God's righteousness. Unfortunately, the followers of these religious practices don't know the difference because they don't read the Bible for themselves. They are left seeking their own righteousness through their works and traditions. All religions do this.

This is exactly what Paul talks about in Romans 10:1–4, which we read earlier. Works-based righteousness is practiced by Roman Catholics and all other forms of religion in which people think they are in the body of Christ, but they are not. Sadly, when people rely on their own works or traditions for salvation, the name they think they have in Heaven is erased. Jesus personally guarantees that only true Christians, the "overcomers" of the world whose names have been written in the Lamb's Book of Life, will never be erased.

> *The one who overcomes will be clothed the same way, in white garments; and I will not erase his name from the book of life, and I will confess his name before My Father and before His angels.*
>
> —Revelation 3:5

The one who overcomes, I will make him a pillar in the temple of My God, and he will not go out from it anymore; and I will write on him the name of My God, and the name of the city of My God, the new Jerusalem, which comes down out of heaven from My God, and My new name.
—Revelation 3:12

The overcomers are the ones who have overcome the world—those who have not given in to the temptations that the world has to offer. They are born-again Christians who overcome the deceptions of the devil and the enticement of the false religion they are in. Overcomers can come out of any of the false religions if God has called and elected them.

And we know that God causes all things to work together for good to those who love God, to those who are called according to His purpose.
—Romans 8:28

If God puts a love for the truth in them and gives them the desire to truly seek Him, and if it is God's will to give them eyes to see and ears to hear the truth, then they will overcome the deceptions of the evil one and be saved. Salvation will not be by their own power because no one can save themselves; salvation comes solely by the power and will of God.

And they overcame him [Satan, the accuser in the context of this Scripture] *because of the blood of the Lamb and because of the word of their testimony, and they did not love their life even when faced with death.*
—Revelation 12:11

Salvation is all done by the blood of the Lamb, Jesus Christ. All a person needs is true faith based on true knowledge. They need to hear the truth, which means they need someone with the willingness and the boldness to speak to them from a biblical perspective. *"So faith comes from hearing, and hearing by the word of Christ"* (Romans 10:17).

So, if you approach your study of the Book of Revelation understanding that it is a prophetic book, and read it over and over again, you will start to recognize the pattern of past, present, and future repeated.

Understanding Revelation's Spiritual Viewpoint

John explains how the Book of Revelation was written: *"I was in the Spirit on the Lord's day, and I heard behind me a loud voice like the sound of a trumpet"* (Revelation 1:10). It is very important to understand that the book of Revelation is written in the Spirit; it is an eyewitness account of things happening in Heaven and on earth from the supernatural perspective. It's not so hard for us to think of Heaven as being supernatural, but it is hard for us to see the world we live in from that same perspective. John, through the supernatural help of Jesus, gives us that perspective and understanding of how the spirit world sees the physical world. The descriptive language used in Revelation is Jesus's way of conveying the supernatural perspective of both Heaven and Earth to us through John's writing. Jesus uses John's account to describe a realm we have not seen and to help us understand.

For John, the experience is as if somebody flipped a light switch on all of creation, turning the world from what we can see in the physical to what Jesus sees in the spiritual. At the flip of a switch, Jesus changes the limits of what John can see, transforming people from what is seen in the physical as just regular people to what is seen in the spiritual. Some are revealed as ugly, horrific, evil monsters when their true nature, their true character, is exposed as Jesus sees them.

For example, when we read the description of "the beast" in Revelation 13:11–18, we naturally imagine that the creature is an ugly monster with fangs and sharp claws and spikes on its back, walking among us on all fours or something like that. We expect a "beast" to be big and hairy and scary. And that is what John is describing because that is what he is seeing, but at the same time, we have to remember that John is in the Spirit, looking down at things on the earth. This beast he is seeing and describing is a man.

From the spirit world, John can see this man's true identity. He can see his spirit. Although the world sees him as a man who talks like a lamb and looks like a lamb, John reveals his true nature—his true character—because John can see him for what he really is. And that is why John describes him as a beast because that's the only way we, in our natural realm, can get some idea of what this person is really like. So, in the natural, physical realm, worldly people will be deceived to think that "the beast" is God's gift to humanity and worship him as a savior. But from the supernatural perspective, this man is an absolute monster, and he can't hide it.

The supernatural realm is where true "reality" exists; it is a greater reality where everyone's true identity—their spirit—is exposed for all to see. Do you wonder what your spirit looks like? In the Spirit, there will be no doubt about which team you are on because your true identity, your true spirit, is known in the spiritual or supernatural realm. On earth, if we are not genuine Christians, we might be able to fake it and get away with making others think that we are generally a good person, but in the spirit world, our true identity will be revealed, and any unforgiven sin will be exposed, proving how lost we are without the forgiveness of sin through Jesus Christ.

Revealing the True Identities Behind False Religions

The book of Revelation reveals the true identities of those behind the world's false religions. It uses figurative language and symbols to reveal the true identity of both people and concepts in our physical world. For example, religion is identified as "the harlot," referring to every "religion" that operates under the title "Christian" or solicits the name of Jesus Christ for profit but is not truly Christian. In the book of Revelation, Jesus refers to every religion as a "whore" or "the prostitute." Now, I know what you're thinking, "Whoa, wait a minute, every religion? What about Christianity? You've gone too far now."

Let me explain. You must understand the difference between religion and biblical Christianity. Religion, every religion, is a personal commitment and relationship to a system. Christianity is a personal commitment and relationship with Jesus Christ. Biblical Christianity is **not** a religion. If you are a born-again Christian, you have every right to be offended if someone calls you religious. You can respond by kindly explaining the difference between religion and Christianity, and boom, you've just become an evangelist.

Worldly Religious Systems

Then one of the seven angels who had the seven bowls came and spoke with me, saying, "Come here, I will show you the judgment of the great prostitute who sits on many waters, with whom the kings of the earth committed acts of sexual immorality, and those who live on the earth became drunk with the wine of her sexual immorality." And he carried me away in the Spirit into a wilderness; and I saw a woman sitting on a scarlet beast, full of blasphemous names, having seven heads and ten horns. The woman was clothed in purple and scarlet, and adorned with gold, precious stones, and pearls, holding in her hand a gold cup full of abominations and of the unclean things of her sexual immorality, and on her forehead a name was written, a mystery: "BABYLON THE GREAT, THE MOTHER OF PROSTITUTES AND OF THE ABOMINATIONS OF THE EARTH." And I saw the woman drunk with the blood of the saints, and with the blood of the witnesses of Jesus. When I saw her, I wondered greatly.

—Revelation 17:1–6

This Scripture uses the analogy of sexual immorality to describe those who use the name of Jesus Christ to seduce people into false religion. *"The great prostitute who sits on many waters"* refers to very large worldwide systems of religion in which even the kings of the earth are practicing her abominations.

In our day, many prominent leaders profess to be attached to some form of religion, and many call themselves "Christian" but do not rely solely on the Bible as their authority. As Bible-believing Christians, how are we to think about such public proclamations of faith?

The phrase *"full of blasphemous names"* refers to all the religions or denominations that use the name of Jesus Christ or take the title of Christian but do not represent true Christianity. In Revelation 17:1–6, all her beauty represents the enticement of the external carnality of prostitution or forms of religious adornment. These religious trappings lure people in with their beautiful buildings, architecture, paintings, artwork, and ridiculously expensive garments. The imagery of these religious trappings is enough to get people in the door and keep them there. The *"gold cup"* in the woman's hand represents all her false teachings in the name of Jesus Christ, which people love to hear so much so, that they become spiritually drunk by them and lose control of their thoughts and actions so that they don't think rationally about what they are participating in mentally, physically, and most importantly, spiritually.

The name written on the woman's head indicates that she has many children; she is the mother of all abominations against true Christianity. There are many forms or denominations to choose from, and she is the mother of them all because she gave birth to them; she is the original false religion from the beginning at the Tower of Babel. The phrase *"drunk with the blood of the saints and with the blood of the witnesses of Jesus"* means that she relishes in the martyrdom of Christ's true followers. The trail of her destruction stretches all the way from the Old Testament, where she killed God's prophets, to the New Testament murder of the apostles, to the massive slaughter during the Reformation, to present-day persecution of Christians, and into the future tribulation where she will kill anyone—not just professing Christians—but anyone who is unwilling to take the mark. John points out that *"the great prostitute"* reigns worldwide for a season. *"And he said to me, 'The waters which you saw where the prostitute sits are peoples and multitudes, and nations and languages'"* (Revelation 17:15).

Isaiah 1:1–31 also talks about the corruption of religion and refers to it as the "prostitute." These abominations to true Christianity seek to make a profit of money, power, and worst of all, souls. Jesus sees what's going on in religion and hates it. In the letter to the church at Thyatira, Jesus says this:

> *Nevertheless, I have a few things against you because you allow that woman Jezebel, who calls herself a prophetess, to teach and seduce My servants to commit sexual immorality and eat things sacrificed to idols. And I gave her time to repent of her sexual immorality, and she did not repent. Indeed I will cast her into a sickbed, and those who commit adultery with her into great tribulation, unless they repent of their deeds. I will kill her children with death, and all the churches shall know that I am He who searches the minds and hearts. And I will give to each one of you according to your works.*
>
> —Revelation 2:20–23 NKJV

Notice that in Revelation 2:20, Jesus calls religion by the name Jezebel. If you do a biblical case study on Jezebel, you will find that she was an Old Testament figure—a wicked queen who practiced horrific sexual immorality and swore to kill God's prophets and anyone who disagreed with her. Her acts are very similar to what we find in the history of the Roman Catholic system. Convincing evidence from comparing Roman Catholicism to the Bible suggests that the spirit of Jezebel is in the Roman Catholic system. Throughout history, Roman Catholic priests have practiced wicked and sexually immoral acts.[1] Church history reveals that, in the name of Christ, Roman Catholic Church leaders tortured and killed countless numbers of people who tried to stand against them and speak the truth— all while claiming to be Christian.[2] For centuries, anyone who disagreed with them and tried to teach the Bible would be cast out of the church, cut off from society, or put them to death,[3] which was and is the ultimate goal of this great prostitute.

Jesus calls the false religious system Jezebel; He says that she *"calls herself a prophetess,"* meaning that her followers take the title Christian, claim to be God's chosen people, and call themselves saints, but they are not appointed or elected by God. They assign the title of "prophetess" to themselves. In the hierarchy of religion, they give titles to themselves and proceed *"to teach and seduce."* In doing so, they add to and take away from God's Word instead of teaching according to the true knowledge of God as revealed in Scripture. They teach their followers to *"eat things sacrificed to idols"* even though that violates Scripture. There is ample documentation showing that Roman Catholic doctrine and teaching led people to participate in a form of sacrifice at every mass, which happens thousands of times a day around the world. For example, Catholic priest and author John O'Brien goes into great detail outlining the procedure and meaning of the Roman Catholic mass. According to his explanation, the Roman Catholic priest performs supernatural feats in bringing Christ down on the altar and offering Him again and again as a sacrifice for the sins of the people.[4] They think they are sacrificing Jesus on their altar to God, but their sacrifice is not going to God but to demons. Moreover, contrary to biblical teaching, their churches are filled with idols in the form of statues, relics, and images in stained glass, which are central to their worship practices and veneration of the saints as set forth at the Council of Trent (1545–1563).[5]

> *What am I saying then? That an idol is anything, or what is offered to idols is anything? Rather, that the things which the Gentiles sacrifice they sacrifice to demons and not to God, and I do not want you to have fellowship with demons.*
> —1 Corinthians 10:19–20 NKJV

Are the Roman Catholics Gentiles or Jews? Of course, they are Gentiles. This verse addresses them directly, along with any other religion that makes sacrifices. God says He hates all their sacrifices and rejects them:

> *I hate, I despise your religious festivals; your assemblies are a stench to me. Even though you bring me burnt offerings and grain offerings, I will not accept them. Though you bring choice fellowship offerings, I will have no regard for them.*
> —Amos 5:21–22 NIV

38

In Revelation 2:20, Jesus says that *"unless they repent of their deeds,"* He will cast them out of His presence. Jesus lets them know that their only way out is to repent. Those who repent are the overcomers. And of course, most of them don't repent because they don't think they need to do so. They believe that their religious rituals cover their sin. Most people who are deceived are far too proud to even think they might need repentance. Jesus says He will cast this prostitute (false religion) into a bed of sickness where she will be tormented in the Great Tribulation along with her followers; He will kill them as an example for all the churches to understand that Jesus knows the mind and heart of everyone. No one gets away with anything, no matter how inconspicuous they think they are.

In Revelation 17:1–6, which we read earlier, John is introduced to the "whore of Babylon," which represents the false religions that are in opposition to the true Christian faith. Research comparing Roman Catholic dogma as defined by the Council of Trent to biblical teaching shows Roman Catholicism to be the worst "whore" of all religions because it prostitutes the name of Jesus Christ more than any other form of religion. Sure, there are many forms of false religion in the world, but none of them use Christianity to seduce people for their money, power, and souls on such a massive scale as Roman Catholicism does. Billions of people are seduced by this harlot, which matches the description of the great prostitute in Revelation 17.

Are you feeling relieved that you're not a Roman Catholic or attached to some other form of religion or cult? Just wait a minute. You're not off the hook just yet. In the next chapter, we will see that Jesus says all denominations and forms of religion that masquerade as Christians while prostituting His name makes Him ill. He says He will vomit because of them and because of their fake love for Him. Specifically, He says, *"So then, because you are lukewarm, and neither cold nor hot, I will vomit you out of My mouth"* (Revelation 3:16 NKJV).

Woke Christianity

Modern-day or "woke" Christianity refers to a whole mass of people who embrace Jesus as everyone's best friend. They love the idea of salvation and going to Heaven, and they take it for themselves, rather than it being a gift from God. Their attitude is like that of the prostitute, which represents false religion, except they don't use the name of Christ for profit; they steal it for themselves. Their kind of spiritual sexual immorality is more like rape. They commit adultery of the gospel by forcing themselves into Christianity without first having Jesus Christ as their personal Lord and then Savior. Currently, the two major offenders of this heinous crime against God are the "HeGetsUs" TV ad campaign and *The Chosen* TV series.

The "HeGetsUs" fake Jesus ad campaign is the worst repeat offender of this horrific offense against the purity of the gospel, and the creators of these ads are doing it on a massive scale. They generalize the Bible, the gospel, Jesus, and the very identity of Christianity so much that in their ads, they make it seem like the door to Heaven is wide open for all to enter. In their eyes, anyone and everyone can be a Christian because "Jesus gets them." All one has to do to be a Christian is to be kind and inclusive of everyone. They condone the belief that love is love; we are to embrace everyone—don't judge, and welcome everyone into the body of Christ because that's what "real" Christians do. So, not only are they feeding fake Christians a fake Jesus that they fully embrace, but they are also feeding true Christians a lie about what they should be like—how they should think, act, react, and interact with the culture around them and how they should view Jesus. Their picture of Jesus is not the righteous vindicator of Holy justice that He is; rather, He is portrayed as a soft, lovey-dovey, all-embracing, woke, in tune with the culture, urban hipster. This is a horrific deception straight out of the pit of hell. It's no wonder Jesus says it makes Him sick. "HeGetsUs" is a perfect example of Satan being disguised as an angel of light.

> *For such people are false apostles, deceitful workers, masquerading as apostles of Christ. And no wonder, for Satan himself masquerades as an angel of light. It is not surprising, then, if his servants also masquerade as servants of righteousness. Their end will be what their actions deserve.*
> —2 Corinthians 11:13–15

The Chosen series also masquerades as an angel of light on television. The program generalizes the Bible, presents an open-ended gospel, and avoids the hard truths about true Christianity. It displays Jesus as a weak man, and a happy-go-lucky jokester, who just loves everyone. He is depicted as a good teacher, and he has some interesting things to say occasionally. Behind the scenes, the producers fully support some of the very things God hates. Gay pride flags can be seen flapping in the breeze hanging from the very camera that is recording the actor who portrays Jesus. If you wonder what God thinks about homosexuality, just read the story of Sodom and Gomorrah (Genesis 18–19). Off the set, the lead actor appears in public and on social media, leading people, not to Jesus, but to dead people they call saints and to Mary. He tells everyone to pray to the dead and to pray to Mary, not Jesus. *The Chosen's* lead actor is a Roman Catholic; the producer is Mormon, which means he doesn't believe in the Jesus of the Bible. He believes Jesus is a created being, not God, and that Jesus and Satan are brothers, and the whole good versus evil thing is just Jesus and Satan having a brotherly dispute over who is the best.

The Chosen is also guilty of violating the second commandment by creating an image of Christ in the form of an actor— someone that people love to watch and fully embrace as a representation of Christ, which he absolutely is not. The second commandment explicitly forbids such portrayals: *"You shall not make for yourself an idol, or any likeness of what is in heaven above or on the earth beneath, or in the water under the earth"* (Exodus 20:4). *The Chosen* creates a likeness of what is in Heaven, Jesus. It gives people a false image of Jesus, who, whether they know it or not, becomes their idol. This can also cause people to subconsciously envision this false image of "Jesus" in their minds when they pray, making him their idol.

So, like the metaphor of spiritual rape, they rob the gospel of its purity and steal the precious gift of salvation through Jesus Christ's shed blood without first having Jesus Christ as Lord of their lives. They neglect Jesus as Lord of their lives, an essential element of the gospel required for people to be transformed from living in sin to living in holiness and devoted to continual sanctification. They reject that part, so Jesus calls them lukewarm, and they make Him sick. If you refer to yourself as a Christian, do not be like these false followers of Christ. Do not live like the world, act like the world, and talk like the world—all while dragging Christ's name along with you through your ongoing, willing, sinful behavior. In doing so, these fake Christians profane the name of Christ. This is a direct violation of the third commandment, which says: "*You shall not take the name of the Lord your God in vain, for the Lord will not leave him unpunished who takes His name in vain*" (Exodus 20:7).

Taking the Lord's name in vain is about more than swearing; it's about living a sinful lifestyle while claiming to be Christian, a representative of Christ. Such blasphemous acts anger the Lord to the point of judgment—not only against the individuals who profane His name but also against entire nations because His holy name is being profaned on a massive scale.

> *And I will vindicate the holiness of My great name, which has been profaned among the nations, which you have profaned among them. Then the nations will know that I am the LORD," declares the Lord GOD, "when I show Myself holy among you in their sight.*
>
> —Ezekiel 36:23

America was once known as having been founded on "Christian" values and biblical morals. But because of religious freedom, America has drifted away from the Bible and biblical morality. The Bible never endorses religious freedom. Why would it? The Bible explicitly says there is only one way—the narrow path (Jesus), only one name—the name above all names (Jesus) by which we must be saved. Religious freedom permits and even encourages people to believe that there are many ways to Heaven. Religious freedom is pragmatism at its best, and it is the death of the exclusivity of Christianity and biblical morality. This spiritual drift has caused us to remove the God of the Bible, the only creator God, from the center of our nation's core beliefs. Now, the world sees Americans as profane, godless, and hypocritical liars who still claim to be Christian even while perpetrating the most horrific offenses against God. This hypocrisy profanes the name of God among all the other nations of the world, provoking God's anger and vindicating His righteous judgment against the nation.

Seeing Reality Through Spiritual Eyes

So, keep it in mind when reading the book of Revelation that the descriptive words reflect what John is seeing in the heavens and on earth from a spiritual perspective. Don't get caught up in the figurative language and imagery, trying to figure things out according to what you understand in our physical world, governed by the laws of physics. Rather, try to see the scenes as John sees them. Imagine that you are in an Imax theater, watching all of creation happen right before you—from beginning to end and back again and everything in between, seeing everything as spiritual. Keep in mind that the figurative words are describing someone's spirit, not an actual physical beast; John is describing an actual physical person on earth, but seeing the person's spirit as a beast, revealing who they truly are. We are seeing the spirit behind certain things, such as organized religion, governmental agencies, or world economics, the way Jesus sees them.

Understanding the Mark of the Beast

Then I saw another beast coming up out of the earth, and he had two horns like a lamb, and he spoke as a dragon. He exercises all the authority of the first beast in his presence. And he makes the earth and those who live on it worship the first beast, whose fatal wound was healed. He performs great signs, so that he even makes fire come down out of the sky to the earth in the presence of people. And he deceives those who live on the earth because of the signs which it was given him to perform in the presence of the beast, telling those who live on the earth to make an image to the beast who had the wound of the sword and has come to life. And it was given to him to give breath to the image of the beast, so that the image of the beast would even speak and cause all who do not worship the image of the beast to be killed. And he causes all, the small and the great, the rich and the poor, and the free and the slaves, to be given a mark on their right

hands or on their foreheads, and he decrees that no one will
be able to buy or to sell, except the one who has the mark,
either the name of the beast or the number of his name.
Here is wisdom. Let him who has understanding calculate
the number of the beast, for the number is that of a man,
and his number is six hundred and sixty-six.

—Revelation 13:11–18

What the Mark Means

The mark of the beast is 666. It is the number of his name.
What is that? What does that mean? It's a gematria, which
Webster's Dictionary defines as "a cryptograph in the form of a
word whose letters have the numerical values of a word taken
as the hidden meaning." In ancient times, and in the original
Hebrew/Aramaic, Latin, and Greek languages, people didn't
have a separate number system; every letter had its own number
assigned to it. Like the Roman numeral X, which is a Latin
letter that can also represent the number 10, the letters and their
numeric values were used interchangeably. The Bible tells us
that if you add up the number of the name of the beast, the total
will be 666.

According to at least one first-century church father, if you
reverse engineer that number using the original Roman numeral
system, 666 spells "Teitan" or, as we would say, "Titan." This is
found in historical writings, which were not included in the Bible,
although they were created about the same time as the Bible.
One person's research supporting this conclusion was Irenaeus,
an early church father and disciple of the Apostle John.[6] Just
because something is not in the Bible doesn't mean it's not true;

46

it simply means that the text was not inspired and, therefore, cannot be taught as the infallible Word of God. Irenaeus's work suggests that Teitan is the name of one of the Nephilim who were the spawn of the fallen angels that raped the women of the earth, as recorded in Genesis 6:1–4.

You may be wondering why I went into such detail about deception and religion earlier. I did so because religious deception is the most dangerous trap that Satan can set. When people fall into Satan's traps of religious deceptions, they become comfortable and satisfied, and they think they need nothing more. The church at Laodicea thought that it was rich and self-sufficient, but Jesus had a different assessment:

> *I know your deeds, that you are neither cold nor hot; I wish that you were cold or hot. So because you are lukewarm, and neither hot nor cold, I will vomit you out of My mouth. Because you say, "I am rich, and have become wealthy, and have no need of anything," and you do not know that you are wretched, miserable, poor, blind, and naked, I advise you to buy from Me gold refined by fire so that you may become rich, and white garments so that you may clothe yourself and the shame of your nakedness will not be revealed; and eye salve to apply to your eyes so that you may see.*
>
> —Revelation 3:15–18

In Verse 17 of this passage, Jesus talks about being rich, using the analogy of financial security as an illustration of spiritual security. He is not talking about being rich with money; He's talking about being rich in the sense of salvation. Salvation is the ultimate form of security; it is better than the security people feel when they have a big bank account. But Jesus tells the Laodiceans that they are actually poor, blind, and naked. In other words, the security they think they have in their false profession of faith, their false religion, is worthless; they can't see the truth that they do not have the pure white garments of God, which signify righteousness and cover sin so that when God looks at us, He does not see our sin because it is covered by the pure and perfect sacrifice of Jesus Christ.

This passage is talking about fake Christians and the religious—those who are either engulfed in religion and have put their faith and fate in the hands of men, or fake Christians who have put their faith and fate in a false profession. This passage calls out those who recited some prayer they heard on TV or made a so-called profession of faith without any heart or lifestyle change. They may be relying on that profession of faith for their salvation, but that profession has not caused change in their life because it was predicated on a lie, a misunderstanding of true salvation, or a fake Jesus, not on true knowledge and faith in Christ. In both cases, these poor people have totally bought into the lie they were fed, resulting in a false assurance of their salvation, which locks them into whatever false belief system they are in.

This is why religious deception is so very dangerous; the consequences are eternal. When people become comfortable and think they need nothing spiritually, they do not repent because they don't think they need to do so.

The Danger of Being Deceived

> *The rest of mankind, who were not killed by these plagues, did not repent of the works of their hands so as not to worship demons and the idols of gold, silver, brass, stone, and wood, which can neither see nor hear nor walk; and they did not repent of their murders, nor of their witchcraft, nor of their sexual immorality, nor of their thefts.*
>
> —Revelation 9:20–21

Because deception is so dangerous, it is Satan's number one weapon of choice. Religious deception is what the mark of the beast is all about. It's about pledging allegiance to a system, a false religion, and a wicked man. This number, 666, is the mark of the religious system because it is the mark of the second beast. The first beast is the controller of governments (Revelation 13:1–10), and the second beast, which is appointed by the first beast, is given power by the first beast as the controller of religion. He creates and establishes a one-world religion and requires that everyone must be part of this system if they are to be a part of society. To identify with this one-world governmental and religious system, everyone has to take the mark on their body—either on their right hand or on their forehead.

The mark is not only to recognize everyone as being a part of their system and not only so a person can buy and sell, but the mark is also to be viewed as a badge of honor. It signifies that everyone honors the death of the first beast. However, we know that the first beast's death is faked because he supposedly rises from the dead. The Bible says, *"Just as people are destined to die once, and after that to face judgment"* (Hebrews 9:27 NIV). And we know that the Bible does not contradict itself and that God is not a God of confusion as it says in 1 Corinthians 14:33: *"For God is not a God of confusion, but of peace."*

The first beast, who is the governmental one-world leader, seems to get killed, and the world mourns for him, but all his power is given to the second beast, who is the one-world religious leader. While everyone is sad and upset and in an uproar about the death of their one-world government leader, the religious leader emerges as one who leads with compassion and seeks unity; he mesmerizes everyone with his speech. As the religious leader, his role is like that of a pope. He unites everyone in honoring the "death" of the first beast whose fake death is designed to get everyone to come together to mourn for him, united with a common purpose.

This second beast sets up an image of the first beast in the place of worship, the temple in Jerusalem, for everyone to worship. He also gives the image the ability to speak. It's possible that he uses artificial intelligence (AI) to make the image appear to be alive. AI makes things seem real to the point that it is almost impossible to tell what's real and what's AI. The beast demands that everyone make their own image of the first beast, so they can have their own idol of him to worship. This makes people worship him as if he is a saint, but this saint will appear to come back to life. Satan gives power to the second beast to deceive people into thinking he has brought the first beast back to life. This is similar to the story I mentioned earlier about human heart DNA being found in a communion wafer.

Satan is always at work deceiving and distracting people from true knowledge; in Revelation 13, he deceives people with a supposed "resurrection" of the dead. The second beast performs signs in the presence of the first beast, as it says in Revelation 19:20:

> *And the beast was seized, and with him the false prophet who performed the signs in his presence, by which he deceived those who had received the mark of the beast and those who worshiped his image; these two were thrown alive into the lake of fire which burns with brimstone.*

So, obviously the first beast is there with him, supporting him, giving him credibility. This is similar to the way that today's world leaders acknowledge the pope, kissing his hand and appearing with him in public and giving him credibility.

In the last days, people will want to worship the "resurrected" beast because their idol appears to have been dead and is alive again, thanks to the satanic deception of a false resurrection. Perhaps Satan will use AI or some form of intelligence to deceive the whole world into worshipping this person that the false prophet has "resurrected" from the dead. The deception starts with him making an image that can speak and putting it in the temple. Then he requires everyone to make their own idol of the image, so they can worship it as a saint, and finally, he performs a deceptive resurrection. They will think that the beast must be Jesus Christ, or at the very least, sent by Him, and they fall for the deception. People will be amazed and mesmerized by all of this, just like my friend was amazed by hearing that heart tissue DNA was found in a communion wafer. People see things like that as a confirming sign; they take it as proof that the deception must be the work of God.

The Bible says that the second beast will be a religious leader who looks like a lamb. Throughout Scripture, the Lamb is always a picture of Jesus. The second beast is Satan's version of Jesus, but, of course, he is a counterfeit. Satan always tries to copy God and God's plan, so the second beast will impersonate Jesus, but he speaks like a dragon. That means that worldly people will see him as God's gift to humanity because he says all the things that people want to hear. He talks unity, love, kindness, liberty, peace, and safety. But according to the Bible and Christianity, his words are from the dragon.

Revelation 19 says he has two horns. In our simple human thinking, we assume that horns coming out of someone's head is a bad thing or evil, but obviously, this is not a person with actual horns. Remember, this is John looking down at the earth from the spiritual realm, describing what he is seeing on earth, in the Spirit. When the Bible talks about horns coming out of someone's head, it is referring to the amount of power and control someone has. This beast has two horns. Jesus has seven horns, referring to the seven churches. The number seven in the Bible always represents perfection and completion.

> *And I looked, and behold, in the midst of the throne and of the four living creatures, and in the midst of the elders, stood a Lamb as though it had been slain, having seven horns and seven eyes, which are the seven Spirits of God sent out into all the earth.*
> —Revelation 5:6 NKJV

In one way, Jesus's power is manifest through His churches. The second beast, also called *"the false prophet"* (Revelation 19:20), has two horns; that is, he has two churches or two religious entities that he unites together as one. It would be like having the pope, who already is a world power, uniting the two largest forms of so-called Christianity in the world today, Roman Catholicism and Protestant Christianity, into one. We have already seen this starting to take shape with the development of an initiative called Evangelicals and Catholics Together, which was formed March 29, 1994, and signed by leaders of both groups. A few pastors on the evangelical side refused to sign the founding document, but many evangelical leaders did sign it along with the pope. This movement may be one explanation of the beast's two horns of power.

The beast's two horns may also represent the conjoining of government and religion. After the first beast establishes a one-world government, the second beast establishes a one-world religion, and the two will be joined together by the second beast. Remember that when the first beast "died," he gave all his power to the second beast, the religious leader, who took charge. The second beast, the one-world religious ruler, will put an end to all the disputes over religion and politics by promising peace and safety and uniting everyone under one religious government. Of course, this turns out to be another one of Satan's traps of deception that many people fall into during the Great Tribulation:

> *While they are saying, "Peace and safety!" then sudden destruction will come upon them like labor pains upon a pregnant woman, and they will not escape.*
> —1 Thessalonians 5:3

At this point in the Great Tribulation, the world's religions and the one-world government have become one entity. All inhabitants of the earth at that time who want to participate in society and have their lives get back to "normal" will take the mark. They won't think anything of it; for the most part, they will have no idea that by taking the mark, they have signed their eternal death warrant.

> *Then another angel, a third one, followed them, saying with a loud voice, "If anyone worships the beast and his image, and receives a mark on his forehead or on his hand, he also will drink of the wine of the wrath of God, which is mixed in full strength in the cup of His anger; and he will be tormented with fire and brimstone in the presence of the holy angels and in the presence of the Lamb. And the smoke of their torment ascends forever and ever; they have no rest day and night, those who worship the beast and his image, and whoever receives the mark of his name."*
> —Revelation 14:9–11

> *And the beast was seized, and with him the false prophet who performed the signs in his presence, by which he deceived those who had received the mark of the beast and those who worshiped his image; these two were thrown alive into the lake of fire, which burns with brimstone. And the rest were killed with the sword which came from the mouth of Him who sat on the horse, and all the birds were filled with their flesh.*
> —Revelation 19:20–21

Those who take the mark of the false one-world religious government system will never see Heaven; identifying with this satanic system is an unforgivable sin. Anyone who does not take the mark will be killed (Revelation 13:15) or die for one reason or another. Think about it. Anyone who does not take the mark will have no access to anything—no food, no water, no gas, no medical treatment, no access to bank accounts, nothing. They will be totally cut off from society. They will die or be killed. Even now, there are people called "preppers" who are prepping to be outcasts from society. Whether they know it or not, they are prepping for the tribulation.

The rapture of the true Christians will kick off the Great Tribulation, which will last seven years—the last seven years of life on earth. Unfortunately, for the preppers, no amount of preparation will keep them alive for very long, three and a half years at best. Many of these people put their faith and fate in the hands of men, a system of religion, or a false profession of faith not based on the true knowledge of biblical Christianity. They will not be raptured because they are not Christians. But they are religious, so they know enough not to take the mark, and by not taking the mark, they know that eventually, they will not be able to buy or sell. So, rather than preparing to be raptured, like born-again Christians, they are preparing to be outcasts because they know they will not take the mark. Some of these are the ones who have a zeal for God but not according to knowledge, which means that a lot of them may have some understanding of the mark of the beast, or they have at the least heard about it and know that they don't want it. However, for most of them, the mark represents the very religion that they are in.

We learned earlier about the spirit of Jezebel, who will either kill people or cast them out of society, in which case they will die anyway. This spirit, which is the very spirit of the system of religion that these people have put their faith and trust in, turns on them, forcing them to take a mark that they don't want. This will cause "preppers" to run and hide, live off the grid, or as they call it, "bug out somewhere." These things will take place during the first three and a half years into the seven-year tribulation, at which point there will be a rebellion.

> *And the ten horns which you saw, and the beast, these will hate the prostitute and will make her desolate and naked, and will eat her flesh and will burn her up with fire. For God has put it in their hearts to execute His purpose by having a common purpose, and by giving their kingdom to the beast, until the words of God will be fulfilled.*
> —Revelation 17:16–17

The ten nations (i.e., "*horns*") will relinquish their power and authority to the first beast, so that they all will be united under the beast and have a common purpose. Together with the "resurrected" first beast, they will hate the prostitute (i.e., the second beast, the leader of false religion, the false prophet) and will strip her of her power, sending her into ruin. The expression *"eat her flesh"* means they will kill all who follow the false prophet. At this point, all religious people will die even if they have the mark, and all who have managed to survive to this point without the mark will be hunted down and killed. The world will finally be completely religion-free. The world and its worldly people will have gotten rid of pesky religion, and most importantly, they will think they have finally gotten rid of God. They will have a totally godless world for about three and a half years—the last half of the tribulation, and evil will have free reign. They will create a world so wicked that God Himself has to come back to stop it before everyone on earth is dead, as it says in Matthew 24:21–22:

> *For then there will be a great tribulation, such as has not occurred since the beginning of the world until now, nor ever will again. And if those days had not been cut short, no life would have been saved; but for the sake of the elect those days will be cut short.*

Desecration of the Temple

Through the second beast, Satan will set up an image in the temple, as mentioned earlier. The Bible says he will set up an image in the temple, and it will be an abomination that causes desolation (Daniel 9). The temple will be an actual physical place in Jerusalem, which has not yet been built. The second beast will set up an image of the first beast there; maybe this will be a form of AI or a clone made in a lab from the first beast's DNA. Who knows what kind of deceptive tactic Satan will use?

But the Bible says we (believers) are also a temple: *"Do you not know that you are a temple of God and that the Spirit of God dwells in you"* (1 Corinthians 3:16)? This passage is talking about saved Christians. But what about those who are not saved? Like those who are left on earth during the Great Tribulation, their temple is either empty, or it has an unclean spirit in it. Jesus made it abundantly clear that many people have unclean spirits in them. Throughout the gospels, He is constantly casting out unclean spirits from people.

During the tribulation, Satan's goal is to set up an image in the temple, but his ultimate goal is to set up his image in **your** temple. He wants to be in you. And he accomplishes that with all who take the mark of the beast; he will be in them. Historically, Satan could only be in one place at a time; he was not an omnipresent being. But using AI and genetic manipulation during the tribulation, he figures out a way to be omnipresent. So, He will be in millions of people at the same time, manipulating them, even controlling their thoughts and their actions and granting them the ability to do certain things and restricting them from doing other certain things.

Revelation 9:6 says, *"During those days people will seek death but will not find it; they will long to die, but death will elude them"* (NIV). They will want to die, but they won't even be able to kill themselves.

The mark is about worshiping and honoring the image, but it's also about **our** image. Consider what the Bible has to say about our image:

> *Then God said, "Let Us make mankind in Our image, according to Our likeness; and let them rule over the fish of the sea and over the birds of the sky and over the livestock and over all the earth, and over every crawling thing that crawls on the earth."*
> —Genesis 1:26

God created man in His own image, but Satan wants people to be in his own image; he is always trying to copy God. He can't create like God does, but he can deceive and manipulate. By taking his mark, people will undergo a transformation on the inside; they will be genetically modified. The transformation will be like a DNA remapping in which their very DNA will be manipulated and changed into something different from what God created. So, they will no longer exist in the image of God but in the image of Satan. A similar deformation of man's God-given nature is the reason why God had to destroy the entire planet the first time in the flood. In Genesis 6:1–13, God describes mankind's rebellion away from His image:

> *Now it came about, when mankind began to multiply on the face of the land, and daughters were born to them, that the sons of God saw that the daughters of mankind were beautiful; and they took wives for themselves, whomever they chose. Then the LORD said, "My Spirit will not remain with man forever, because he is also flesh; nevertheless his days shall be 120 years." The Nephilim were on the earth in those days, and also afterward, when the sons of God came into the daughters of mankind, and they bore children to them. Those were the mighty men who were of old, men of renown.*
>
> *Then the Lord saw that the wickedness of mankind was great on the earth, and that every intent of the thoughts of their hearts was only evil continually. So the Lord was sorry that He had made mankind on the*

earth, and He was grieved in His heart. Then the Lord said, "I will wipe out mankind whom I have created from the face of the land; mankind, and animals as well, and crawling things, and the birds of the sky. For I am sorry that I have made them." But Noah found favor in the eyes of the Lord.

These are the records of the generations of Noah. Noah was a righteous man, blameless in his generation. Noah walked with God. And Noah fathered three sons: Shem, Ham, and Japheth.

Now the earth was corrupt in the sight of God, and the earth was filled with violence. And God looked on the earth, and behold, it was corrupt; for humanity had corrupted its way upon the earth. Then God said to Noah, "The end of humanity has come before Me; for the earth is filled with violence because of people; and behold, I am about to destroy them with the earth.

When His creation is no longer in the image that He created it to be, God has to destroy it. This is not limited to people; it applies to all His creation. Think about how man has genetically modified plants and animals, creating corrupt seed. God destroys it all in the end just like in the flood, only this time it is destroyed with fire. Fire destruction is permanent; even the elements will melt, as Peter says in 2 Peter 3:10 (NKJV):

But the day of the Lord will come as a thief in the night, in which the heavens will pass away with a great noise, and the elements will melt with fervent heat; both the earth and the works that are in it will be burned up.

This chapter has presented an in-depth discussion of the mark of beast. For those who would like to know more about the meaning of the word *mark*, I included a word study in the Appendix.

You Are Commissioned

Urgency of the Gospel Message

At the beginning of *Pray Before Reading*, we prayed to the Father in Heaven for wisdom. With the knowledge you gained from reading this book, you should have a better understanding of what Christianity is and is not. But most important of all, you have the Bible. What are you going to do with what you have learned? You see, Christianity was never meant to be a solitary affair or hidden inside you, or to be self-centered, or to be received by self-will. Once you come to the knowledge of salvation and are blessed with the wisdom of understanding and, by God's grace, you have become a born-again Christian, it is no longer about you and your salvation or your eternal destiny. Rather, it is about others and their salvation and their eternal destiny; they need to know the truth about salvation based on true knowledge understood with godly wisdom. This is the essence of the great commission— to go forth and make disciples; this is the purpose and meaning of life for Christians. In Matthew 28:19, Jesus commands us to: *"Go, therefore, and make disciples of all the nations, baptizing them in the name of the Father and the Son and the Holy Spirit."*

We are to spread the good news of salvation by the blood of Christ to the ends of the earth. This is why Christians are here on Earth, and not raptured away, not yet. Jesus prayed to God the Father on our behalf: *"I am not asking You to take them out of the world, but to keep them away from the evil one"* (John 17:15). He didn't pray for us to be taken to Heaven as soon as we are saved and become Christian; He prayed for our divine protection.

If you are a Christian, you have been recruited by God to go on mission, serving Him as His Christian warrior and defender of truth. When you hear the word *missions*, what is the first thing that comes to mind? Is it traveling to a faraway place where there is no clean water to drink or a comfy bed to sleep in? Most likely. While going on a mission trip to a faraway place is a wonderful thing to do, and those people definitely need the Word of God and to be shown the passion of a Christian's love for others, we are not all called to endeavor in such a mission. As a matter of fact, very few are, and even fewer actually go. When I say, "God has called you to go on mission," I'm talking about reaching those who are all around you—right where you live.

Earlier, we looked at what the world has become, how Satan is masquerading around as an angel of light, and how so many people are deceived into thinking they are Christians when they are not. You can go on mission right where you live. You have been recruited to share the gospel with which we have been blessed and to spread the good news to anyone and everyone you meet, starting with your own family.

Use this book as an evangelistic tool to share with others. Maybe you know someone stuck in a religious system or someone who says they are a Christian even though their lifestyle does not reflect that claim, or someone who is lost and needs to have their questions answered. Give them this book or invite them to read it with you. If you are a believer, you have an important role to play in spreading the gospel message:

> *You are the salt of the earth; but if the salt has become tasteless, how can it be made salty again? It is no longer good for anything, except to be thrown out and trampled underfoot by people.*
>
> —Matthew 5:13

Jesus uses salt as a metaphor to portray the important role that Christians have in the world. In biblical times, salt was a valuable preservative; even today, we use salt to preserve things. When Jesus says we are the salt of the earth, He means that we are, by the power of the Holy Spirit living in us, the preservation of righteousness on earth. Without Christians, as we learned earlier, the earth will become an extremely evil, dark place.

In addition to being salt, Christians are to let the light of Christ shine through them into this dark world. Jesus said:

> *"You are the light of the world. A city set on a hill cannot be hidden; nor do people light a lamp and put it under a basket, but on the lampstand, and it gives light to all who are in the house. Your light must shine before people in such a way that they may see your good works, and glorify your Father who is in heaven."*
>
> —Matthew 5:14–16

You are called to live like a true Christian, a representative of Christ here on Earth. A true Christian will not live like the heathens, the worldly people, and participate in ungodly things. Instead, we are to separate ourselves from a worldly lifestyle:

"Therefore, COME OUT FROM THEIR MIDST AND BE SEPARATE," says the Lord. "AND DO NOT TOUCH WHAT IS UNCLEAN; And I will welcome you. "And I will be a father to you, And you shall be sons and daughters to Me," Says the Lord Almighty.
—2 Corinthians 6:17–18

Your separation from them and their worldly lusts and activities will be a testimony to your claim to Christianity and salvation. Apostle Paul describes the Christian life this way:

But I say, walk by the Spirit, and you will not carry out the desire of the flesh. For the desire of the flesh is against the Spirit, and the Spirit against the flesh; for these are in opposition to one another, in order to keep you from doing whatever you want. But if you are led by the Spirit, you are not under the Law. Now the deeds of the flesh are evident, which are: sexual immorality, impurity, indecent behavior, idolatry, witchcraft, hostilities, strife, jealousy, outbursts of anger, selfish ambition, dissensions, factions, envy, drunkenness, carousing, and things like these, of which I forewarn you, just as I have forewarned you, that those who practice such things will not inherit the kingdom of God.
—Galatians 5:16–21

You will be a living example of what it means to be a Christian, not in isolation, but for all to see that you are different from others because of the choices you make and the life you live.

The knowledge given to us as believers through the Word of God, the Bible, is a gift from God to be shared through the fruit of the Spirit working in you, so that it may be multiplied. We are to walk in the Spirit so that God may be glorified and that He may glorify Himself through us.

> *But the fruit of the Spirit is love, joy, peace, patience, kindness, goodness, faithfulness, gentleness, self-control; against such things there is no law. Now those who belong to Christ Jesus crucified the flesh with its passions and desires. If we live by the Spirit, let's follow the Spirit as well. Let's not become boastful, challenging one another, envying one another.*
> —Galatians 5:22–26

In the parable of the talents, Jesus explains the importance of what we do with what we receive:

> *"For it is just like a man about to go on a journey, who called his own slaves and entrusted his possessions to them. To one he gave five talents, to another, two, and to another, one, each according to his own ability; and he went on his journey. The one who had received the five talents immediately went and did business with them, and earned five more talents. In the same way the one who had received the two talents earned two more.*

But he who received the one talent went away and dug a hole in the ground, and hid his master's money.

"Now after a long time the master of those slaves came and settled accounts with them. The one who had received the five talents came up and brought five more talents, saying, 'Master, you entrusted five talents to me. See, I have earned five more talents.' His master said to him, 'Well done, good and faithful slave. You were faithful with a few things, I will put you in charge of many things; enter the joy of your master.'

"Also the one who had received the two talents came up and said, 'Master, you entrusted two talents to me. See, I have earned two more talents.' His master said to him, 'Well done, good and faithful slave. You were faithful with a few things, I will put you in charge of many things; enter the joy of your master.'

"Now the one who had received the one talent also came up and said, 'Master, I knew you to be a hard man, reaping where you did not sow, and gathering where you did not scatter seed. And I was afraid, so I went away and hid your talent in the ground. See, you still have what is yours.'

"But his master answered and said to him, 'You worthless, lazy slave! Did you know that I reap where I did not sow, and gather where I did not scatter seed? Then you ought to have put my money in the bank, and on my arrival I would have received my money back with interest. Therefore: take the talent

away from him, and give it to the one who has the ten talents.'

"For to everyone who has, more shall be given, and he will have an abundance; but from the one who does not have, even what he does have shall be taken away. And throw the worthless slave into the outer darkness; in that place there will be weeping and gnashing of teeth.

—Matthew 25:14–30

The man at the center of this parable is a picture of Jesus; He has gone away on a long journey (i.e., ascended into Heaven) and entrusted us with His possessions. He has left us with precious possessions that include the true knowledge found in the Bible and the godly wisdom to understand it. The talents refer to the amount of knowledge, understanding, and wisdom God gives to us, based on our individual abilities and our desire to seek Him. That's why Jesus said, *"Seek and you shall find."* Seek Him through His word, and He will let Himself be found.

And he went out to meet Asa and said to him, "Listen to me, Asa, and all Judah and Benjamin: the Lord is with you when you are with Him. And if you seek Him, He will let you find Him; but if you abandon Him, He will abandon you."

—2 Chronicles 15:2 NASB2020

The only limitation of revelation from God is our desire and commitment to seek Him in His Word.

The amount of revelation given to a person is in direct correlation with the amount of seeking that person does. The moral of the story is to whom much knowledge and wisdom are given, much is expected; those who do nothing with what they are given will lose even what little they had. Therefore, if you receive revelation and wisdom from God through reading His Word but don't share it with others, the Word won't multiply and produce more good fruit. If you do nothing with it, you will not retain it nor reap any benefits from knowing it or be productive in the work of God.

But Jesus invites us to abide in Him so that we can be fruitful:

> *Remain in Me, and I in you. Just as the branch cannot bear fruit of itself but must remain in the vine, so neither can you unless you remain in Me. I am the vine, you are the branches; the one who remains in Me, and I in him bears much fruit, for apart from Me you can do nothing. If anyone does not remain in Me, he is thrown away like a branch and dries up; and they gather them and throw them into the fire, and they are burned.*
> —John 15:4–6

Remain in the Word of God, and He will remain in you, and you will bear much fruit. When the Word is implanted in good soil, it will produce in abundance. In the parable of the sower, Jesus says, *"But others* [seeds] *fell on the good soil and yielded a crop, some a hundred, some sixty, and some thirty times as much"* (Matthew 13:8). The implanted seed is the *"word of the kingdom,"* or the knowledge from God through His word, the

Bible. When it is implanted in good soil (i.e., true Christians), it produces a bounty for the Lord. The bounty is realized in souls saved through the hearing of the truth of the Word of God.

True Christians have been called to live a life transformed by the Word of God, to be representatives of Christ here on earth, and to spread the true and full gospel of Jesus Christ to all the nations. We are to share the gospel with everyone—friends, family, and strangers alike. No matter the cost. True love for one's neighbor means loving someone enough to tell them the truth, even if it causes uncomfortable moments, tension, or anger. Even if it costs you the relationship or even your own life. Jesus said to count the cost.

> *Now large crowds were going along with Him, and He turned and said to them, "If anyone comes to Me and does not hate his own father, mother, wife, children, brothers, sisters, yes, and even his own life, he cannot be My disciple. Whoever does not carry his own cross and come after Me cannot be My disciple. For which one of you, when he wants to build a tower, does not first sit down and calculate the cost, to see if he has enough to complete it? Otherwise, when he has laid a foundation and is not able to finish, all who are watching it will begin to ridicule him, saying, 'This person began to build, and was not able to finish!' Or what king, when he sets out to meet another king in battle, will not first sit down and consider whether he is strong enough with ten thousand men to face the one coming against him with twenty thousand?*

*Otherwise, while the other is still far away, he sends a
delegation and requests terms of peace. So then, none
of you can be My disciple who does not give up all his
own possessions.*
—Luke 14:25–33

This doesn't mean you have to sell everything you own and buy a megaphone to yell at people in the streets. Jesus is saying there is a price to pay for being a true Christian in this world and that we shouldn't bother starting if we can't commit to seeing it through to the end. Don't be a fake Jesus follower, like many people are. If you are going to be a true Christian, you will have to abandon your old sinful life and commit everything in your life to the Lord. Everything He blesses you with, you must entrust back to Him, trusting that He knows what's best for you.

This may mean abandoning some of your old relationships if necessary. However, Christians don't usually abandon people; they are more likely to abandon us because we choose to follow Christ. As you continually decline your friends' invitations to participate in ungodly things (Galatians 5:19–21) because of your Bible-based convictions, one of two things will happen. They will either see this change in you and want to know more and possibly be saved as well, or eventually, they will stop inviting you, and the relationship will fade away.

If you are going to be a true Christian, you may even be hated by some. But Jesus has these words of wisdom for us:

*If the world hates you, you know that it has hated
Me before it hated you. If you were of the world,
the world would love you as its own; but because*

you are not of the world, but I chose you out of the world, because of this the world hates you.
—John 15:18–19

The Call to Faith in Christ Jesus

If you are not a Christian, know that God loves you and wants you in His kingdom someday and that He has provided a way for you. No matter who you are, what you have done, or where you are from, God loves you so much that He provided a way for all sinners and all people to be reconciled to Him. That way is Jesus Christ:

- *Jesus said to him, "I am the way, and the truth, and the life; no one comes to the Father except through Me"* (John 14:6).
- *"As it is written: 'There is no righteous person, not even one'"* (Romans 3:10).
- *"For all have sinned and fall short of the glory of God"* (Romans 3:23).
- *"But God demonstrates His own love toward us, in that while we were still sinners, Christ died for us"* (Romans 5:8).
- *"For the wages of sin is death, but the gracious gift of God is eternal life in Christ Jesus our Lord"* (Romans 6:23).
- *"For with the heart a person believes, resulting in righteousness, and with the mouth he confesses, resulting in salvation"* (Romans 10:10).

What would stop you right now from asking Jesus to save you—to transform your life so that you are no longer a slave to sin but a servant of the Lord Jesus Christ? I don't mean perfection in this life, because we all fail, because we all live in a sinful world, but I'm referring to a new direction—a change from walking in darkness to walking in the light with Jesus as your guide. The Christian life means walking with Jesus—one step at a time. You may not see an immediate and full transformation, but don't give up on God because He will not give up on you if you continue to seek Him in His Word.

The Apostle Peter says, *"The Lord is not slow about His promise, as some count slowness, but is patient toward you, not willing for any to perish, but for all to come to repentance"* (2 Peter 3:9). It is not God's will that you should perish in hell, but rather, it is His will to save you from the consequences of sin, which is eternal death in hell. The penalty for dying in unforgiven sin is death, and it will take an eternity to pay the penalty—which means we can never pay for it. There is only One who can pay for our sin; that is Jesus Christ, God's son. Why can Jesus Christ pay for our sin? Because He was born of a virgin and lived a perfect, sinless life, making Him a perfect sacrifice to God on our behalf.

- *"Therefore the Lord Himself will give you a sign: Behold, the virgin will conceive and give birth to a son, and she will name Him Immanuel"* (Isaiah 7:14).
- *"Now the birth of Jesus the Messiah was as follows: when His mother Mary had been betrothed to Joseph, before they came together she was found to be pregnant by the Holy Spirit"* (Matthew 1:18).

The virgin birth is important because this is the only way that Jesus could have been born sinless. This means He was not born of ordinary generation but of supernatural generation. That is, He did not inherit His father's sin, which every person born of ordinary generation naturally inherits from Adam; we are naturally born sinners. Thus, everyone dies because *"the wages of sin is death but the gracious gift of God is eternal life in Christ Jesus our Lord "* (Romans 6:23). Jesus lived a sinless life, making Him the spotless Lamb who takes away the sin of the world.

"The next day he [John the Baptist] *saw Jesus coming to him, and said, "Behold, the Lamb of God who takes away the sin of the world""* (John 1:29)! He takes away the sin of the world for all who believe in Him and call on His name. He offered Himself as a holy and righteous sacrifice to God for our sins as He paid for them in full on the cross when He died. Then He rose from the dead on the third day, defeating sin and death; He then appeared to many witnesses who saw His resurrected body, touched Him, and ate with Him, as recorded in Scripture.

- *"Then He said to Thomas, 'Place your finger here, and see My hands; and take your hand and put it into My side; and do not continue in disbelief, but be a believer'"* (John 20:27).
- *"Jesus said to them, 'Come and have breakfast.' None of the disciples ventured to inquire of Him, 'Who are You?' knowing that it was the Lord. Jesus came and took the bread and gave it to them, and the fish likewise. This was now the third time that Jesus revealed Himself to the disciples, after He was raised from the dead"* (John 21:12–14).

The Christian believes that salvation is through Christ's work alone of living a perfect life, being God incarnate, being the perfect sacrifice for our sins, being raised from the dead to defeat death and sin, and overcoming the world to set us free from sin. Salvation is not by our works or anything we do because there is nothing that we can do to save ourselves. If we could save ourselves by good works, the cross would be made worthless. Jesus's sacrifice is sufficient because He is perfect, spotless, blameless, holy, and righteous, and His death is justification for us who believe in order that we will be able to stand before God and be deemed worthy because of Him. His sacrifice for our salvation needs no assistance from us. If it did, it would no longer be perfect because we are imperfect, sinful, lost, helpless, and hopeless. He is perfect; therefore, His sacrifice is the one and only work that can be accepted by the holy, righteous, and just God of all creation.

Believing in that and knowing it to be true, we repent of our sins and cry out to God for mercy and forgiveness:

- *"But the tax collector, standing some distance away, was even unwilling to raise his eyes toward heaven, but was beating his chest, saying, 'God, be merciful to me, the sinner'"* (Luke 18:13)!

- *"And there is salvation in no one else; for there is no other name under heaven that has been given among mankind by which we must be saved"* (Acts 4:12). Repent of sin, which means to turn away from it. Resist it, and it will lose its hold on you.

- *"Submit therefore to God. But resist the devil, and he will flee from you"* (James 4:7). That is repentance. That is the repentant Christian who will enter Heaven one day.

A Prayer of Salvation

Call on His name, the name above all names, Jesus Christ.

Lord,

Come into my life; send Your Holy Spirit to live in me, to change me, and make me whole. I no longer want to be a slave to sin but a servant of You. Help me. By Your power, give me the wisdom, guidance, and understanding to live my life obeying all that You command for me as a Christian, so that I can come out from the world and be separate, in order to glorify You, God, in all that I do for Your name's sake, for Your glory, and Your Kingdom come.

Amen.

Closing Prayer

Dear Father in Heaven,

We started this book with a prayer for wisdom. We are pleading before You, God, the only source of true wisdom, asking You to bless us with Your wisdom and understanding and with the humility to accept it because Satan and his servants are masquerading as angels of light, deceiving whomever they can. We know that at the end of this life, there are only two options: Heaven or hell.

In the world, there are only two types of people: born-again Christians and everybody else. There are two marks: the mark of the beast, 666, and the mark of God, the cross. And we've come to a crossroads of asking ourselves, which one do we want. Oh, Father in Heaven, do not let us be deceived. We seek Your wisdom so that we will not be deceived into thinking we have the right mark or deceived into thinking that we have a name in Heaven, but do not.

Dear God, open our eyes so we can see the truth and all that You want to reveal to us through Your written Word. God, open our ears so we can hear the truth, the full truth, and be saved. We do not want to walk in darkness, but to walk in the Light, so that we will not stumble. God, change us because You are the only One who can. It's not programs or treatment or therapy or self-will that changes people. Although those things are not all bad and may help people in a sense, we know that the only source of true change is a new heart. And the only One who can do that is You, God. Lord God, give us a new heart. Remove our heart of stone so that we can truly love You and serve You with our lives. May our lives be a living testimony of Your amazing grace and Your saving and transforming and limitless power. Do Your work in and through us.

May Your will be done and Your kingdom come on earth as it is in Heaven.

Amen.

Appendix: Word Study— Mark or Tav in Hebrew

T he word *mark* is an interesting word in its original Ancient Hebrew language. *Mark* comes from the Hebrew/Aramaic word "Tav." It's interesting because of where it first pops up in the Old Testament.

Note the use of the word *mark* in God's handling of Cain after he kills his brother:

> *And the Lord said to him, "Therefore, whoever kills Cain, vengeance shall be taken on him sevenfold." And the Lord set a mark on Cain, lest anyone finding him should kill him.*
>
> —Genesis 4:15

The next use of *mark* that I want to call to your attention appears in a prophecy from Ezekiel. Remember that true prophecy speaks in terms of what was, is, and is to come. In this Scripture passage, Ezekiel is seeing events in his time and in the time yet to come, the Great Tribulation:

Then He cried out in my presence with a loud voice, saying, "Come forward, you executioners of the city, each with his weapon of destruction in his hand." And behold, six men came from the direction of the upper gate which faces north, each with his smashing weapon in his hand; and among them was one man clothed in linen with a scribe's kit at his waist. And they came in and stood beside the bronze altar.

Then the glory of the God of Israel ascended from the cherub on which it had been, to the threshold of the temple. and He called to the man clothed in linen at whose waist was the scribe's kit. And the LORD *said to him, "Go through the midst of the city, through the midst of Jerusalem, and make a mark on the foreheads of the people who groan and sigh over all the abominations which are being committed in its midst." But to the others He said in my presence, "Go through the city after him and strike; do not let your eye have pity and do not spare. Utterly kill old men, young men, female virgins, little children, and women, but do not touch any person on whom is the mark; and you shall start from My sanctuary." So they started with the elders who were before the temple. He also said to them, "Defile the temple and fill the courtyards with the dead. Go out!" So they went out and struck and killed the people in the city. And as they were striking the people and I alone was left, I fell on my face and cried out, saying, "Oh, Lord GOD! Are You going to destroy the entire remnant of Israel by pouring out Your wrath on Jerusalem?"*

Then He said to me, "The guilt of the house of Israel and Judah is very, very great, and the land is filled with blood, and the city is full of perversion; for they say, 'The LORD has abandoned the land, and the LORD does not see!' But as for Me, My eye will have no pity nor will I spare, but I will bring their conduct upon their heads."

Then behold, the man clothed In linen, at whose waist was the scribe's kit, reported, saying, "I have done just as You have commanded me."

—Ezekiel 9:1–11

It is important to note that in both passages of Scripture, the word for mark is the Hebrew word *tav*. Here, Ezekiel writes about the destruction of Israel, God's people, because of their falling away. It is his current reality and a prophecy. Remember that true prophecy from God consists of three parts, and it works like this: what was, what is, and what is to come. Ezekiel is a great prophet of God. He is writing down what he sees as all three at the same time: historical events, current events, and future events.

Ezekiel prophesies exactly what will happen in the end during the Great Tribulation. Satan copies what God reveals in this Scripture. He puts his mark on people, and those who do not take his mark are killed. God puts His mark on people to preserve righteousness; Satan puts his mark on people to preserve and promote evil.

> *After these things I saw four angels standing at the four corners of the earth, holding the four winds of the earth, that the wind should not blow on the earth, on the sea, or on any tree. Then I saw another angel ascending from the east, having the seal of the living God. And he cried with a loud voice to the four angels to whom it was granted to harm the earth and the sea, saying, "Do not harm the earth, the sea, or the trees till we have sealed the servants of our God on their foreheads." And I heard the number of those who were sealed. One hundred and forty-four thousand of all the tribes of the children of Israel were sealed.*
> —Revelation 7:1–4 NKJV

So that's 12,000 from each of the twelve tribes, and each one of them receives the mark of God. These are the elect from Mathew 24:22 that we read earlier. They are the ones about whom God said that He would cut the days of evil short for their sake else all would die. They get the *tav* of God.

Revelation 14:1 confirms this tally: *"Then I looked, and behold, the Lamb was standing on Mount Zion, and with Him 144,000 who had His name and the name of His Father written on their foreheads."* This verse uses the same word as when the angels with the seal of God were told to go and mark or tav God's people, the Jews, specifically the 144,000, so that they would not get the tav of the beast, so they would be preserved for God. They are the remnant.

That word, "tav," is extremely important to understand because of its significance throughout the entire Bible. Ever since the beginning, people have been marked for one reason or another.

In Revelation 1:8 (NKJV), Jesus tells the Apostle John, "I am the Alpha and the Omega, the Beginning and the End," says the Lord, "who is and who was and who is to come, the Almighty." But He said "Alpha and the Omega" in Hebrew/Aramaic because that's the language that he spoke. How do we know that? Because we have Scripture that tells us so.

> *We all fell to the ground, and I heard a voice saying to me in Aramaic, 'Saul, Saul, why do you persecute me?. . . "Then I asked, 'Who are you, Lord?' 'I am Jesus, whom you are persecuting,' the Lord replied.*
> —Acts 26:14–15 NIV

In Revelation 1:8, Jesus uses Aleph and Tav as an illustration to show us that He is the first and the last. He is also using it to demonstrate to us that He literally is the beginning and the end of all things. Together, those two words, Aleph and Tav, spell "The Word." In English, it would be pronounced, *et'* or *eet'*. That word pops up in some very interesting places in the Bible. For instance, when John wrote his Gospel, he started it by saying:

> *In the beginning was the Word, and the Word was with God, and the Word was God. He was with God in the beginning. Through Him all things were made; without Him nothing was made that has been made. In Him was Life, and that Life was the light of all mankind. The Light shines in the darkness, and the darkness has not overcome it.*
>
> —John 1:1–5 NIV

What word is John talking about? The following diagram shows the first verse of the Bible in both Hebrew and English. It consists of seven words in Hebrew—the number of perfection.

Gen 1:1

בראשית ברא אלהים את השמים ואת הארץ

the earth	and	the Heaven	'eet	God	created	In the beginning
haa'aarets	w'eet	hashaamayim		Elohiym	baaraa'	bree'shiyt

BETHEL CHURCH

Here, we find that the *Aleph* and *Tav* are in the middle of the first verse of the Bible. Jesus, right from the beginning, is found directly in the middle of the first verse in the Bible in Hebrew. The significance of the word *tav* can be a bit confusing, but it is also mind-blowing once you piece it all together.

Hieroglyphics is the root language of Arabic. Hebrew and Arabic are from the same root language and are interchangeable in some respects. The Old Testament scribe Ezra spent his lifetime transcribing the writings of Moses, the first five books of the Bible, which Moses wrote in hieroglyphics. That is, he wrote in symbols. We would commonly call it cavemen writing, like what we see on the History Channel on the side of caves or on stone tablets. In the original paleo-Aramaic language of hieroglyphics, *Alpha* and *Omega* or *Aleph* and *Tav were* represented by two symbols. Alpha was represented by an ox, and Omega was represented by a cross.

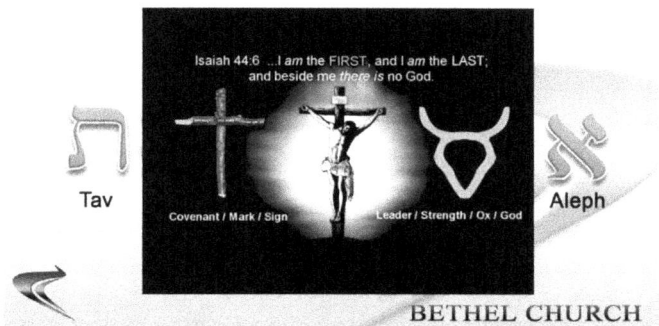

The word *tav* or Omega was originally represented by the symbol for the cross—essentially, the "Mark" of the cross. So, think about the Scriptures we just read and all the instances in which the word for mark showed up as "tav." The people who were getting the "Mark" of God, the seal of God, were getting the sign of the cross marked on their foreheads. God was symbolically telling them, thousands of years before it happened, that He would save them through His son, Jesus

Christ and His sacrifice. In the human dispensation of time, the physical realm, this didn't take place until thousands of years later, but in the supernatural realm, it had already happened.

Alpha refers to the ox to be sacrificed, the sacrificial ox. In Revelation 1, Jesus was saying "I am the sacrifice who was crucified." Think about this: Moses wrote the first verse in the Bible in hieroglyphics. God was conveying through Moses from the beginning that Jesus was and is the sacrifice to be crucified. For more insights into these matters, you may find it helpful to refer to Part 1 of a study of the Book of Revelation presented at Royston Bethel, Yorkshire, UK, by Pastor Dave Jones.[7]

Acknowledgments

Thank you to my wife Beth, for always being there for me and helping me.

And thank you to Tim and Sara Kunick, for their support in this project.

Notes

1. Tim Roemer, "After Catholic Church Sex Abuse Cover-ups, We in the Pews Must No Longer Simply Pray & Pay," *USA Today,* November 23, 2018, https://www.usatoday.com/story/opinion/2018/11/23/catholic-church-sex-abuse-coverups-reforms-pennsylvania-grand-jury-column/2060850002/.

2. John Foxe, *Foxe's Book of Martyrs* (Bridges-Logos, Inc, 2001). Originally published in 1563 by John Day.

3. Foxe, *Book of Martyrs.*

4. John O'Brien, *The Faith of Millions: The Credentials of the Catholic Religion* (Our Sunday Visitor, 1974).

5. J. Waterworth, ed. and trans., *The Council of Trent: The Canons and Decrees of the Sacred and Ecumenical Council of Trent,* (Dolman, 1848), https://www.papalencyclicals.net/councils/trent.htm.

6. J. David Stark, "Irenaeus on 666 and 616" (blog), https://www.jdavidstark.com/irenaeus-on-666-and-616/.

7. Dave Jones, YouTube channel @RoystonBethelTV (Royston Bethel TV) "Revelation Bible Study, Part 1 (Introduction, Chapter 1), https://www.youtube.com/watch?v=Kk4LtJ6JxWw.

www.ingramcontent.com/pod-product-compliance
Lightning Source LLC
Chambersburg PA
CBHW051432090426
42737CB00014B/2941